Arms and Armour

Elspeth Graham

OXFORD
UNIVERSITY PRESS

OXFORD
UNIVERSITY PRESS

Great Clarendon Street, Oxford OX2 6DP

Oxford University Press is a department of the University of Oxford.
It furthers the University's objective of excellence in research, scholarship,
and education by publishing worldwide in

Oxford   New York

Auckland   Cape Town   Dar es Salaam   Hong Kong   Karachi
Kuala Lumpur   Madrid   Melbourne   Mexico City   Nairobi
New Delhi   Shanghai   Taipei   Toronto

With offices in

Argentina   Austria   Brazil   Chile   Czech Republic   France   Greece
Guatemala   Hungary   Italy   Japan   Poland   Portugal   Singapore
South Korea   Switzerland   Thailand   Turkey   Ukraine   Vietnam

Oxford is a registered trade mark of Oxford University Press
in the UK and in certain other countries

Text © Elspeth Graham 2006

The moral rights of the author have been asserted

Database right Oxford University Press (maker)

First published 2006

British Library Cataloguing in Publication Data

Data available

ISBN 978-0-19-917949-7

7 9 10 8

Printed in China by Imago

Acknowledgements

The publisher would like to thank the following for permission to reproduce
photographs: **p5** DK Images, tr Museum of London, **p11** Heritage Museum, **p12** DK Images, br
Heritage Museum, **p13** DK Images, **p16**c British Museum, t & b DK Images, **p19** Corbis/Ludovic
Maisant, **p20** DK Images, **p21** Heritage Museum, **p23**c British Museum, **p27**t Getty/AFP,
b Getty/David McNew, **p28** Corbis/Hulton Archive, **p29**t Corbis/Bettmann, b Getty Images

Illustrations by: **p7**br, **p11**, **p25**b Leo Broadley, **p4**, **p6**t, **p8**, **p9**r, **p10**, **p13**b, **p14**t, **p19**, **p21**c,
p22, **p23**, **p24**, **p25**t, **p26** Dan Crisp/The Bright Agency, **p6**l, **p7**, **p9**l, **p14**b, **p15**, **p17**, **p18**,
p21t, **p24**tr Paul Young/Artist Partners

Cover by Paul Young/Artist Partners

Design by Chrome-Dome Design

Every effort has been made to contact copyright holders of material reproduced in this book. If notified,
the publishers will be pleased to rectify any errors or omissions at the earliest opportunity

Contents

The first weapons

The stone had been carefully chosen. It fitted the hand well. Now it had to be struck, very carefully, with a hard hammer-stone to flake off small bits of flint from the edges. Then it would have to be ground and polished with smaller stones or some deer antler until it was very sharp. It would be the shape of a teardrop…

It's a sad fact that since the earliest times human beings have been dreaming up ways to hurt each other. This means that they've also had to work out ways of protecting themselves from being hurt.

Thousands and thousands of years ago, in the early Stone Age, people learnt that by chipping hard stones, like flint, they could make a rough cutting edge. These sharpened stones could be used for killing and skinning animals. They could also be used for defence and to attack others.

By the late Stone Age, people had worked out how to lash a handle onto the sharpened stones, and so the first simple axes and spears were invented.

Tools like this were being used by 40,000 BC.

By 10,000 BC wooden spear-throwers had been devised to increase a spear's range.

Harpoons were made from deer antlers for stabbing fish. The first bows and arrows were being fired.

With the discovery of metals – first copper, then bronze and later iron – the making of tools and weapons was changed completely. With metal axes, people could chop down a tree quite quickly. With metal tipped arrows and spearheads, humans became far more dangerous. The first real warriors had arrived.

Metal tools like these were first used in Europe about 6,000 years ago.

Early armour

The earliest warriors wore little protection – at most, tunics made of leather or thick quilted cloth. 5,000 years ago, Sumerian soldiers wore heavy, leather cloaks with metal studs.

Scales and mail

Some of the earliest real armour was made from scales – small separate plates sewn onto cloth or leather to make a flexible coat. (Maybe the idea came from lizards or crocodiles!) Scales were made of iron, bronze or even slices of horses' hooves.

Mail was made by linking or riveting metal rings together. It was more flexible than scale-armour; it could be formed into hoods, gloves and leggings. Mail was worn by soldiers in many parts of the world.

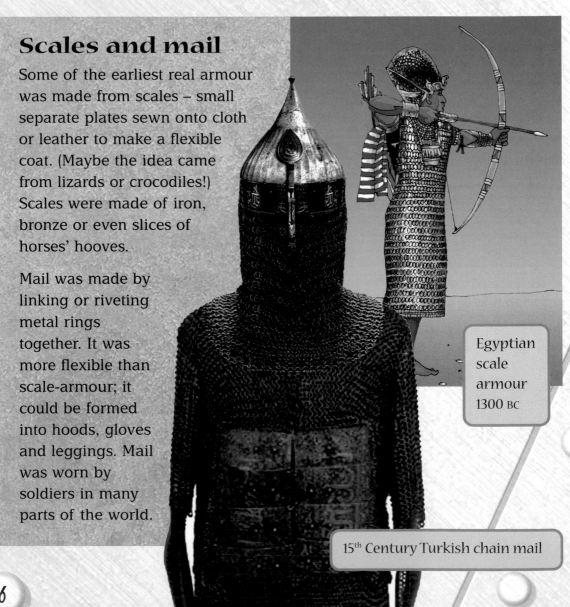

Egyptian scale armour 1300 BC

15th Century Turkish chain mail

Early missiles

They had run as far as they could run. They turned, exhausted, to face their pursuers. The ground around them was rough and broken. They bent and gathered up handfuls of stones…

Flying stones

Among the first and crudest weapons were stones hurled at the enemy. One of the earliest devices for propelling stones further, harder and with more accuracy was the slingshot.

The boomerang

The Aboriginal war boomerang didn't come back – and it wasn't meant to! Made of hard heavy wood, it could bring down an animal or an enemy 150 metres away. Boomerangs were used in Africa, America and in India, as well as in Australia.

boomerang

Deadly spears

Spears are one of the most ancient and versatile of weapons. They can be used for throwing and stabbing, and for self-defence – they can keep an enemy out of arm's reach.

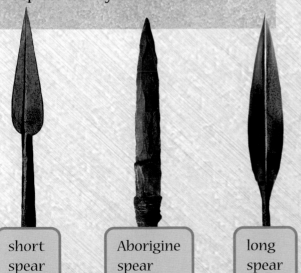

short spear

Aborigine spear

long spear

Tread carefully

'Crows' feet' were nasty little gadgets thrown into the path of advancing cavalry in order to damage the horses' feet and make them lame.

Bows and arrows

The ring of horsemen had surrounded the enemy. Now the leader lifted his powerful bow. He held it in his left hand, pushing it forwards; his right arm pulled the string all the way back, past his ear. He was ready to loose the first arrow…

The bow was the first real long-range weapon. Every civilisation has used it for hunting and fighting.

Mighty Mongols – horsemen from hell

Tough, fast and brutal, the Mongols were possibly the most terrifying army the world has ever seen. Brilliant horsemen and cunning warriors, they conquered Asia and invaded Europe 700 years ago.

Scythian archers

The Scythians were ferocious, hit-and-run mounted archers. If their enemies weren't overwhelmed by the first hail of arrows, the Scythians rode a safe distance and prepared for another mass attack. They dominated much of Central Asia 2,500 years ago.

A Mongol bow of bamboo, wood, horn and sinew.

Getting to the point

The first arrowheads were chips of flint. Later, when people learned to forge metal, there were many different designs: narrow heads for penetrating mail; chisel heads to pierce armour; barbed ones to cause maximum damage to flesh.

narrow arrowhead

barbed arrowhead

chisel arrowhead

Native Americans

Like the Mongols, The Plains Indians of North America were brilliant horsemen and archers. Their skill at buffalo hunting on their hardy, agile ponies also made them a fearsome enemy against people. Their favoured tactic was the lightning-fast, hit-and-run raid.

It was mine

The arrows of some Indian **clans** could be identified by their unique designs. At least you'd know who shot you...

Hot frogs!

Some rainforest tribes obtained poison for their arrows by 'sweating' poisonous frogs over a fire and wiping the arrowheads on the frogs' skin...

...and pipes!

The blowpipe was used by a number of American peoples. The light darts used with the blowpipes were too small to cause death – that's why they usually had poisoned tips.

The medieval knight

Europe, 550 years ago. Covered from top to toe in fine steel, a knight watches the battlefield below him. His horse is armoured too and looks like a terrifying metal unicorn. A more lightly-armoured footman holds the knight's standard – the flag around which his troops will rally during the bloody chaos of the battle…

Armour agenda

1 Bits and pieces
A sophisticated suit of armour consisted of over 200 steel plates, joined or hinged together. There could be as many as eight separate plates just between the toe and the instep of one foot.

2 Heavy duty
A suit of 'white armour' made from high quality steel weighing between 20 and 30 kilograms. That's fairly heavy; but with the weight evenly distributed over his body, a knight was quite mobile. He wasn't the lumbering dinosaur people often imagine.

3 Nimble knights
By the 15th century, armour was so skilfully made that knights could move about quite easily. They could even dance – and there's a medieval drawing of a knight in full armour doing a cartwheel!

Designer labels

Today, the Italian city of Milan is a centre of the world of fashion, where designers, like Armani, show off their latest creations. Things were much the same in medieval times. The craftsmen of Milan produced some of the best and most stylish armour in Europe. For the fashionable knight, Milan was *the* place to shop.

The price of style
In 1441, Sir John Cressy bought a suit of Milanese armour. For the same money he could have bought a house or a herd of cattle.

Longbow versus...

Long lines of soldiers face each other. They've waited in the rain for a long time. Between them the newly ploughed earth has turned into a sea of mud. Then a cloud of arrows fills the air with a dull scream. Wounded horses throw their riders into the mud and the mayhem begins...

Longbow

The longbow, capable of firing armour-piercing arrows over a distance of 300 metres, was the ultimate English weapon during the 14th and 15th centuries. A good archer could launch an arrow every five seconds.

Robin Hood

Longbows were not only deadly, they were cheap and easily carried – ideal weapons for **fugitive** outlaws like the legendary Robin Hood.

Agincourt

The longbow's greatest success was at the battle of Agincourt in 1415. The French army was cut to pieces by English archers firing so many arrows that 'it was as if a thick fog had hidden the sun'.

crossbow

Crossbow

The crossbow was a short bow mounted on a wooden **stock**. Its bowstring was pulled back under great tension often using a two-handled crank, and then released by a trigger. Its power was deadly, easily piercing steel armour from 100 metres away.

Bowman protection

Crossbowmen were vulnerable targets during the relatively slow business of loading, so they sheltered behind big wooden shields called *pavises* and were protected by archers or **pikemen**.

William Tell

Switzerland's national hero, William Tell, was a crossbowman. For refusing to recognize the Austrian rulers of his country, he was forced to shoot an apple from his son's head. Luckily for Tell Junior, he succeeded!

Pros and cons

The crossbow was immensely powerful and accurate, but it was more complicated and expensive than the longbow, and had a slower rate of fire, so most medieval armies used both weapons side-by-side.

Bashers and...

Mud, blood, the screaming of people and animals, metal hacking at metal: the battlefield was a scene of nightmarish chaos...

To put a fully-armoured person out of action, you needed to pierce the steel with something sharp, or land a mighty blow with something heavy. Some hand weapons did both.

Violent Vikings

Vikings were lightly-armoured, lightning-fast and savage raiders who fought on foot. As well as swords and axes, they fought with hammers – the favoured weapon of their war-god, Thor.

Heavy metal

Maces were heavy metal clubs with ribs or spikes to maximize damage. Dual-purpose war-hammers had a blunt end for smashing helmets and a steel-piercing blade.

Flailing around

A particularly nasty weapon was the flail – an iron ball attached to a staff by a length of chain.

Zulu clubs

Zulu war-clubs were called *knobkerries*. Folklore says that there was a limit on the size of the club head – it had to fit inside its owner's mouth!

stabbers

Roman military dagger

The Roman dagger, worn at the left hip, had a wide, double-edged blade. Heavy knives of the same design were still being manufactured in Italy in the 16th century.

African dagger

This weapon from Zaire was so heavy that European explorers thought it was meant to be dropped from a tree onto the enemy's head!

Malay kris – curvy killer

The wavy-bladed *kris* is found in many parts of South East Asia, including Malaysia and Indonesia. Krises vary greatly in size and style according to their particular places of origin.

Indian khanjar

The Moguls, Muslim warriors who invaded India in the 16th century, introduced many Persian-style weapons, including this curved, double-edged *khanjar*.

Gurka knife

The Gurkas of Nepal are proud, tough soldiers. Their traditional knife, the *kukri*, is a lethal weapon; it's also handy for hacking through dense jungle.

A blood-thirsty blade

Legend says that before being returned to its sheath, the kukri must taste blood – its owner's blood, if need be…

Cutters and...

The sword is one of the oldest and most universal weapons.

Roman short sword

The short thrusting sword used by Roman infantry was called the *gladius*. (That's where the word *gladiator* comes from.)

Swords of the Samurai

Japanese Samurai swords had a flexible core of iron inside layers of hard, sharp steel. The ancient way to test a newly-forged blade was on the body of a condemned criminal.

Swords were often handed down from generation to generation. During the Second World War (1939–1945) some Japanese officers carried swords which had belonged to their families for over 400 years.

Leg-biter

Throughout history, swords were so highly valued that they had their own names. Viking swords had names like *Blood-drinker* and *Leg-biter*. In the middle ages swords were given names like *Joyous*, *Precious* and *Glorious*.

slashers

Claymore

The classic Scottish sword was the claymore, or great sword. A long, heavy, two-handed weapon, it was swung in great circular sweeps, building up an irresistible **momentum**.

From field to battlefield

In the middle ages, peasants were **conscripted** into armies during times of war. Often they had nothing to fight with other than tools they brought with them from their farms: axes, scythes, pitchforks and the like. Several weapons are developments of these tools.

The long-handled billhook was designed to prune trees and cut hedges, but it proved useful against mounted soldiers and became commonplace on the battlefield.

The wickedly beautiful *igorot* axe from the Philippines was originally a versatile jungle-clearing tool, but was also horribly effective in a fight.

Axes, of course, are equally useful for cutting down trees and people. Battle axes were used throughout the world and came in all shapes and sizes. This blade and pick version, made of steel, is an Indian *tabar*.

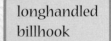

longhandled billhook

igorot

tabar

Shields

The shield is the oldest form of self-defence (apart from running away, of course). It can also be a weapon, a badge of office, a means of identification, or a work of art.

A shell of shields

The Romans used their curved shields in ingenious ways. The *testudo* (tortoise) formation of interlocking shields was used when attacking fortresses.

Shield materials

Shields come in an amazing variety of shapes, sizes and materials. European shields were usually of wood covered in leather – effective in stopping arrows. In many parts of the world, shields were made of stiffened animal hide on a wooden frame. In different parts of Africa, shields were made of wickerwork, or rhino skin, or even cotton, packed so densely that it could stop a bullet.

hide   wicker   wood

Tribal I.D.

The Maasai people of East Africa paint their leather shields in varying symbolic patterns of red, white and black. Each shield identifies the warrior's age, family, home, battle-group and bravery in battle.

Heraldry

In battles and tournaments, armoured **combatants** identified themselves by the colours and symbols on their shields. These signs developed into the complex identification system we call heraldry.

Each **aristocratic** family had its own coat of arms, based on the shield shape. When members of different families married, their arms were combined on one shield. They might then add a crest,

a motto, mythical beasts supporting the shield and all sorts of bits and pieces – ending up with a design that was very fancy indeed.

Helmets

The Samurai warrior prepared for battle and for death. One of the terrifying things about the Samurai was that they often chose to die. Disgrace was unbearable; death in battle or by choice was preferable. Death always included beheading. Before the battle the Samurai would burn incense in his helmet, so if his head was taken the smell of it would please his victor.

As everyone knows, the first thing you protect is your head. But helmets do more than protect: they can make you seem taller and more powerful, and a helmet which is also a mask can terrify your enemy.

Samurai

The Samurai helmet or *kabuto* had a hole in the top for the Samurai's hair-knot to pass through. The Samurai also wore a face-mask; this fastened the helmet more securely to the head and gave the warrior an even more frightening appearance.

Vikings

Vikings are often depicted wearing horned helmets, but there is no real evidence that they did. Their helmets resembled Norman ones, with narrow nose-pieces and chain-mail neck guards.

Style wars

Ornamental parade armour in the late medieval period grew more and more bizarre. Helmets sprouted birds' beaks, or turned into fantastic animal masks.

Over the top

The full helmets called *great helms* masked the face completely. To help identify themselves to their troops, 14th century commanders wore elaborate crests perched on top of their helmets, usually in the form of animals featured in their coats of arms. They were made of boiled and moulded leather, wood and plaster, gilded in the knight's colours.

What a spectacle!

This helmet, straight out of a horror-film, was a present to Henry VIII from the Holy Roman Emperor. It was fitted with spectacles because Henry was short-sighted!

Animals at war

There were many mounted men. The horses moved forwards quickly. Most were mares chosen because they wouldn't **nicker** to the enemy's own horses. They attacked with *speed, surprise* and in near *silence*. The best of the mares were courageous and didn't flinch from the spear thrusts…

Thousands of years ago, horse-soldiers began to protect their mounts with leather, scale or mail armour. But other animals wore armour too.

A living tank

Few sights can have been more fearsome than the ultimate war-machine of the Indian Princes: six tonnes of charging elephant, coated in steel plate and mail, its tusks fitted with savage, curved blades. Elephants sometimes carried a small wooden castle or *howdah*, from which arrows – or even lightweight cannon – could be fired.

Hannibal

In 218 BC, the **Carthaginian** general, Hannibal, achieved the near-impossible by leading his army and 50 elephants across the Alps into Italy. The astounded Roman army was heavily defeated.

Horse armour

By the late 15th century, European horse-armour – or *barding* – had become very sophisticated. But it was heavy and slowed a horse considerably.

Elsewhere in the world, horse-armour was lighter, made of padded cloth or studded leather.

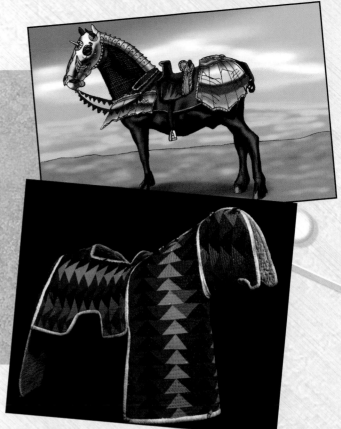

Dogs of war

Dogs have been going to war for a long time. 4,000 years ago, the Babylonian army used fierce hounds – gigantic, brutally strong, mastiff-like dogs. The Romans favoured powerful British mastiffs. In medieval battles armoured dogs with spiked collars were used to attack opponents' horses.

Hot dogs

The Romans had a particularly clever and nasty trick involving dogs. The poor beasts were fitted with harnesses which carried pots of burning tar; then they were made to dash about inside the enemy camp, causing fire and general havoc.

Early firearms

At the order 'fire' the soldier pressed the trigger of his weapon. The smouldering match descended onto the gunpowder inside the pan of the firearm. The explosion sent him staggering backwards in a cloud of black smoke…

Gunpowder was known in Europe as early as 1300. It was first used in crude cannon and mortars and for undermining castle walls.

King James' mistake

King James II of Scotland was so proud of his cannon that, at a siege in 1460, he paraded in front of them – while they were firing. And that was the end of him!

The end of armour?

During the 16th century, firearms began to change the nature of warfare. Mounted soldiers still fought in full plate-armour, which could resist pistol shot. But it was useless against fire from heavy muskets which could cut down armoured horsemen long before they had a chance to use their **lances** and swords. It was the beginning of the end for the noble armoured knight.

Covering fire

Like crossbows, early guns were very slow to load. This put gunners at risk, and they had to be protected by those age-old weapons – the pike and the bow.

Matchlock and wheel-lock

Primitive guns were fired by poking a burning fuse (the *match*) directly into the gunpowder.

Later matchlock muskets did this mechanically by means of a trigger, so that both hands could be used to steady the gun.

Later still, wheel-lock firearms did away with the match altogether. The trigger spun a metal wheel against a chip of **iron pyrites**, producing sparks which ignited the powder.

Where am I?

One of the problems with early gunpowder was that it produced clouds of dense choking smoke. After firing a **volley**, a troop of gunners might have no idea at all of what was going on around them.

Modern armour

By the late 17th century, firearms had made the aristocratic, magnificently armoured knight **obsolete**. But armour did not disappear – it evolved.

Knights in the city

Today, many vicious battles are fought in the streets of cities, and police in their riot gear can strangely resemble medieval knights and men-at-arms. Tough plastic shields and visors and flame-resistant clothing protect them from stones and petrol bombs. Their 'non-lethal' arms include batons, plastic bullets and tear gas.

Bullet-proof vests

Today's soldiers often wear armoured vests to protect them against bomb-fragments and bullets from handguns; but they give very limited protection against high-powered rifles.

Armoured vests consist of layers of different materials: hard **ceramic** and plastic to deflect bullets; 'soft' armour to absorb bullets; and 'trauma shields' to soak up and spread the shock of a bullet's impact.

Biological weapons

To be protected against deadly chemical and biological weapons, modern soldiers must be covered completely in airtight suits; the air they breathe has to be filtered through a mask.

In the balance

The full equipment carried by a modern soldier actually weighs *more* than a suit of armour worn in battle 500 years ago.

Armoured transport

Medieval knights used to protect the horses they rode with armour.

Armour plating still protects ships, planes and land vehicles that are used today.

Armoured vehicles

Leonardo da Vinci made sketches of an armoured car back in 1482. It was moved by the power of the soldiers inside it who also fired muskets through slits in the side.

The *Charron* armoured car was developed in 1904. It had a petrol engine and was protected by plates of armour 6 millimetres thick. Wooden wheels were protected by steel plates. It had a maximum speed of 18 kilometres per hour (11 miles per hour).

Armoured protection is used for combat vehicles by the military. It is used by civilians to protect **VIPs** like politicians and royalty.

Tanks

A tank is a **tracked** armoured fighting vehicle designed to destroy enemy ground forces by direct fire. It has the heaviest armour on the battlefield and is a fearsome weapon.

The first tanks were developed 100 years ago and used the **chassis** of a petrol-driven tractor combined with armour plate protection and were armed with machine guns.

After being successfully used in the First World War, tank designs were improved and developed into the sophisticated machines that they are today.

Helicopters

In 1500 Leonardo da Vinci sketched his ideas for helicopters.

Helicopters are also known as 'rotary wing aircraft'. The main **rotor** can be tilted, and this creates a current of air to lift the aircraft into the sky. The small rotor at the back keeps the helicopter flying level and straight.

Because helicopters can take off and land **vertically** they are used to transport troops, stores and casualties.

The first helicopter lifted a person from the ground in 1907. Some were flown in the First World War, but they didn't come into regular use until after the Second World War. Military helicopters have protective armour and armoured crew seats.

Quiz

Try this quiz about the arms and armour in this book. If you are stuck on a question, the Index on page 32 may help you find the information you need.

1 Why did blowpipe darts need to be poisoned?

2 On the battlefield, what was the importance of a knight's standard?

3 Knights in full armour couldn't walk unaided. True or false?

4 If you'd wanted to buy really stylish armour in medieval times, where would you have gone shopping?

5 How many arrows could a good longbowman fire in one minute?

6 Why did crossbowmen always have *quarrels*?

7 Why was it dangerous to have William Tell as your dad?

8 What was Thor likely to hit you with?

9 Why would you think carefully before drawing your *kukri*?

10 Were *Joyous* and *Leg-biter* names given to
    (a) swords   (b) horses?

11 Where might you find a *howdah*?

12 What was *barding*?

13 Where would you wear a *kabuto*?

14 Why would a modern soldier wear soft armour?

Glossary

aristocratic – belonging to a wealthy or ruling class

carhaginian – someone from the ancient state of Carthage in North Africa

ceramic – pottery

chassis – base frame of a motor vehicle

clan – a group of people related by blood or marriage

combatant – someone involved in a fight

conscripted – made to join an army or armed forces

fugitive – someone who is running away, or has been banished or exiled

iron pyrites – a mineral that strikes a flame, 'firestone'

lance – long wooden pole with sharp metal ends held by horsemen charging at full speed

momentum – the build up of force of movement

nicker – one of the sounds that a horse makes – a low whinny

obsolete – out of date or no longer of use

pikemen – soldiers armed with pikes – long wooden poles with a sharp metal head

rotor – the rotating part of a motor

sinew – a strong cord that connects muscle to bone, taken from an animal's body

stock – the strong wooden body to which the working part is attached

tracked – having continuous metal belts fitted over cogged wheels, to enable the vehicle to travel over rough ground.

vertically – going straight up or down

VIP – very important person

volley – to fire a number of firearms, or bows, all at once

Index